CW01621849

St Antholin's Lectures

Charity Lecture 2008

# From Life's First Cry

## John Owen on infant baptism and infant salvation

Lee Gatiss

ISBN 978-0-946307-70-8



Published by the Latimer Trust
PO Box 26685
London N14 4XQ

www.latimertrust.org

*No guilt in life, no fear in death;*
*this is the power of Christ in me;*
*from life's first cry to final breath*
*Jesus commands my destiny.*
*No power of Hell, no scheme of man*
*can ever pluck me from his hand:*
*till he returns or calls me home,*
*here in the power of Christ I'll stand!*

## Contents

## Setting the Scene

With the great Assembly of puritan Divines sitting in Westminster, a sermon was preached each morning in Westminster Abbey. One such sermon from 1644 by Mr. Stephen Marshall, minister of Finchingfield in Essex, sparked something of a controversy when another minister chose to publish a long and weighty response to it. The sermon, itself somewhat longer than usual, was part of a series on the Ten Commandments, the Lord's Prayer, the Creed, and the Sacraments and took as its subject the doctrine of infant baptism. Marshall outlined the basic historical, theological, and biblical case for the practice.[1] Mr. John Tombes, who was fast gaining a reputation as one who was against infant baptism, read Marshall's printed sermon and decided it must be answered.

Tombes had already been turned down for a prestigious preaching post[2] by a committee on which the influential Marshall sat, because of his views on this subject. As 'the archetypal Anglican Antipaedobaptist'[3] he was particularly concerned to justify his own position in a church and nation which had long accepted the practice of baptising the children of believers. Tombes' response was about three times the length of Marshall's sermon, and was bound along with some of his other polemical writing on the subject, the first of many such

---

[1] S. Marshall, *A Sermon of the Baptizing of Infants* (London, 1644). On Marshall's reputation and influence as a preacher, see W. Barker, *Puritan Profiles* (Fearn, Ross-shire: Mentor, 1999), pages 120-127.

[2] Preacher for the Honourable Societies of the Temples, in London.

[3] M. T. Renihan, *Antipaedobaptism in the Thought of John Tombes: An untold story from Puritan England* (Auburn, MA: B&R Press, 2001), page 47.

published works to come from his pen over the next few years.[4] Marshall replied to Tombes's response, and soon others weighed in too. Thus began a long and spirited exchange of views amongst the English puritans of the mid-seventeenth century concerning the place and privileges of children in the church.

This debate over infant baptism certainly made waves in Oxford, where John Owen, 'Prince of Puritans' was Dean of Christ Church (1651-1660) and Vice-Chancellor (1652-58). At the annual academic convocation in 1652, for example, Henry Savage delivered a dissertation specifically against John Tombes's views. Moreover, in 1654, Tombes was appointed as a 'Trier', charged with the examination and approval of ministers. This was a high profile role, and would naturally have drawn attention to Tombes and his distinctive theological convictions from the universities where new clergy were being trained by men such as Owen (also a Trier).[5] It is into this rhetorical and theological context that we can place Owen's own work on infant baptism, which is (unfortunately) undated.[6] Whether it

---

[4] J. Tombes, *An Examen of the Sermon of Mr. Stephen Marshal about Infant Baptisme* (London, 1645). In total he wrote at least 14 books touching on the issue of baptism according to Renihan, *Antipaedobaptism*, page 66. His paper on the issue presented to the Westminster Assembly probably accounts for Marshall's verbosity in outlining the case for infant baptism in his sermon; as Renihan, page 142 comments, "Polemicising with Tombes brought about tedious work for all parties involved"!

[5] See Renihan, *Antipaedobaptism*, pages 44-45.

[6] The text in *The Works of John Owen* is reprinted from an edition of his 'Sermons and Tracts' only published posthumously in 1721 and perhaps never intended for publication at all. The next treatise in the *Works*, "A vindication of two passages in Irenæus against the exceptions of Mr. Tombs" (pages 263-265 of Volume 16), is a direct reply to Tombes's *Antipaedobaptism* Part 3, section 89, pages 760-762 which was published in 1657. If this 'vindication' was originally appended to *Of Infant*

originates from the 1640s, perhaps as a position paper sent to the Westminster Assembly,[7] from the 1650s when the debate was evidently current in Oxford, or from the post-Restoration period when Richard Baxter also continued to wield his prolific pen against Tombes,[8] we cannot say with certainty. Yet his only work devoted to the sacrament of baptism, a short treatise of about 2400 words simply called *Of Infant Baptism*, is a classic example of puritan theological exegesis and polemical argumentation.

The doctrine of infant baptism, especially its denial by Anabaptists, was a major catalyst for the development of covenant theology in the 16th and 17th centuries, a movement in which Owen was very much involved. Yet it was not merely a scholastic exercise that led the greatest mind amongst the puritans to consider the related subjects of infant baptism and infant salvation. Owen and his first wife had 11 children together, only one of whom survived past infancy.[9] Sadly, such

---

*Baptism*, as seems possible judging from the final point made there about "particular testimonies may be pleaded and *vindicated* if need be" (emphasis mine), then it is not unlikely that he completed both around 1657-1658.

[7] Tombes had sent a short *Exercitation* on the subject to a committee of the Assembly. Owen himself was not a member of the Westminster Assembly, but may well have been asked by members for his opinion.

[8] Tombes moved to a chapel-at-ease in Bewdley, where he would not be required to baptise anyone, in 1649 (Renihan, *Antipaedobaptism*, page 52 footnote 44). According to *Reliquiae Baxterianae* (London: Matthew Sylvester, 1696), Part I, page 96, Tombes vigorously pursued Baxter, his near neighbour, for a public debate which finally took place in January 1649/50. Baxter's first work dedicated to the issue was *Plain Scripture Proof of Infants Church-Membership and Baptism being the arguments prepared for... the publick Dispute with Mr. Tombes at Bewdley* (1650).

[9] Two of his sons died in a plague in 1655, just before the date I have suggested Owen wrote *Of Infant Baptism*, according to P. Toon, *God's Statesman: The Life and Work of John Owen* (Exeter: Paternoster, 1971),

immense tragedy was not unusual or exceptional for his time,[10] which meant that the puritans generally gave more thought than perhaps we do today to issues of infant salvation. They did not always have the luxury of time to consider whether to baptise their children or not.

We turn our attention then to the pithy and tightly woven argument which Owen makes for infant baptism. He has four sections to his argument, but in true puritan fashion the fourth section has eight major sub-points and several sub-points have sub-sub-points! So I will try to clarify how it all fits together as we proceed. My first point deals with Owen's first three sections, lines of argument I-III.

## 1. What is the question?

Owen begins in the style of an Oxford disputation by defining very carefully the question to be debated. He clears the ground for his more positive arguments by denying three things. First, he says, the issue is not "whether professing believers... not baptised in infancy, ought to be baptised." This, he states, is an

---

page 63. His daughter Mary had died in July 1647 aged only three weeks (Toon, page 38 footnote 3).

[10] For example, A. G. Matthews, *Calamy Revised* (Oxford: Clarendon Press, 1988 [1934]), pages 13-14 records that Samuel Annesley had 24 children, only three of which survived him. One of these was Susanna, the mother of John and Charles Wesley (and 16 others!). D. A. Thompson, *Baptism, Church and Society in Modern Britain* (Milton Keynes: Paternoster, 2005), page 1 narrates something of the story of the 17th century Revd Isaac Archer who lost eight of his nine children in infancy, and as many as three out of ten children in puritan New England did not reach their first birthday according to C. A. Brekus, "Children of Wrath, Children of Grace: Jonathan Edwards and the Puritan Culture of Child Rearing" in M. J. Bunge (ed.), *The Child in Christian Thought* (Cambridge: Eerdmans, 2001), page 316.

uncontroversial truth, confessed by all Christians. Presumably the wording of the Great Commission in Matthew 28:18-20 was clear enough in its insistence that disciples of Jesus ought to be baptised, even if in actual fact that is not universally the case.[11]

Second, Owen continues, neither is the debate about whether faith and repentance should precede baptism in such disciples. It obviously should, and Owen would insist on pastors taking great care over this, so as not to baptise adult converts without being sure their profession of faith is genuine. He claims to be more assiduous and careful about this than most antipaedobaptists, for whom admission to baptism was something to be extremely scrupulous about. By clarifying that this is not the main issue, he rules out any simplistic appeal to verses (such as Acts 8:12) which speak of repentance or faith coming before baptism as if they settled the issue of baptizing infants. To pile up quotations, from either the Bible or great theologians of the past, showing that faith did or should precede baptism *in adults* is not pertinent to the question of infant baptism, since it is perfectly consistent with the paedobaptist position.[12]

---

[11] I have met some Christians, converted and nurtured through the Salvation Army for example, who have never been baptised, and there are always others who have 'not gotten around to it yet'. Whilst it is gloriously true that baptism is not strictly necessary for salvation, it is clearly abnormal in New Testament terms to neglect baptism altogether (see *Westminster Confession* 28.5). After all, there are many things which are 'not strictly necessary for salvation' but which are either beneficial to growth in faith, or matters of simple obedience to God's word (e.g. Bible reading, prayer, the Lord's Supper).

[12] Owen possibly has Tombes in his sights here since he argued thus in *An Examen of the Sermon of Mr. Stephen Marshal*, page 153, making much of a list of several verses in which either John the Baptiser or the Apostles baptised adults after a profession of faith and/or repentance. For a modern example of this kind of argument, see R. H. Stein, "Baptism in

Third, Owen denies that all infants should be baptised. In other words, he and his fellow paedobaptists do not wish to argue that every child born into the world without exception ought to be baptised. Some children, he says, ought not to be baptised, i.e. those "whose parents are strangers from the covenant." This is the first mention in the argument of that important concept of 'the covenant', to which we will return again as Owen develops his case. It is sufficient to note at this stage that Owen was not in favour of indiscriminate baptism nor would he have approved of a policy of baptising the children of anyone who happens to live in the parish (whether they are committed to Christ and his covenant people or not). As we will see later, Owen was of the view that some of those born outside the covenant who died in infancy were actually elect and saved; yet that did not mean they should be baptised (since God alone knows those who are his) or that any child could be baptised simply in the hope that they might be one of the elect. Baptism was, then, part of the outward administration of the covenant, a

---

Luke-Acts" in T. R. Schreiner & S. D. Wright (eds.), *Believer's Baptism: Sign of the New Covenant in Christ* (Nashville: B&H Academic, 2006), pages 35-66. Since the context of Luke-Acts must be the whole of Scripture (breathed out by the same divine author), to consider a doctrinal question settled by appeal to narrative examples in only a section of the whole would be premature, even if the examples *were* directly relevant to the issue at hand. Whilst this kind of 'biblical theology' description of what a particular corpus of biblical material says can be useful, unless we move from "what does Luke-Acts say" to a consideration of how that coheres with the rest of the Bible and how it is relevant to the systematic question being asked, it is ultimately misleading and cannot be normative. The rest of the Schreiner-Wright volume does attempt this. However, it is to be feared that many would simply conclude that "if in Luke-Acts baptism is for adults who have heard the gospel and professed faith, then infant baptism cannot be right." It is that logical fallacy which Owen is here addressing.

sign to be given only to those whose profession of saving faith and repentance was judged sincere, and to their children.[13]

So, Owen has cleared away three false definitions of the question he has chosen to discuss, in order to focus the dispute more precisely. The issue for him is not whether believers who weren't baptised in infancy should be baptised - they should. It is not whether faith and repentance should come before baptism in such converts – it should. And it is not whether all infants are to be baptised indiscriminately – they should not. Therefore he concludes that "the question is only concerning the children or infant seed of professing believers who are themselves baptized". And the question is, should *they* be baptised?

It is not pedantic or 'scholastic' to narrow the question down in the way Owen did. Clarity is vital in such debates, especially where passions can often run high. It is also important not to forget at the beginning of his argument that Owen believes in adult 'believer's baptism' (or credobaptism) as much as any antipaedobaptist.[14] Indeed, as a keen supporter of

[13] See *A Declaration of the Faith and Order Owned and practised in the Congregational Churches in England, Agreed upon and consented unto By their Elders and Messengers in Their Meeting at the Savoy, October 12, 1658* (London, 1658) section 29.4. This is identical to *Westminster Confession* 28.4 except that it strengthens the limitations on who can be baptised: believers and their children, "and those only" (the last three words being added at the Savoy). Owen was instrumental in drawing up this 'Savoy Declaration', which is a lightly edited version of the *Westminster Confession*, and so the revisions made are significant when considering Owen's own views, especially if my view (above, footnote 6) of the date of *Of Infant Baptism* is correct.

[14] The official statistics show that the number of adult baptisms in the Church of England in 2006 was 9,300, an increase of 11% since 2002, demonstrating that a paedobaptist denomination can also in a sense be a credobaptist one. So where I use the term 'antipaedobaptist' (Tombes's

missions to the un-reached people groups of Great Britain and Ireland who worked and prayed for the propagation of the gospel, he would have taken great joy in the baptism of such new converts.[15] This is a healthy reminder that a firm belief in infant baptism need not involve neglecting the evangelisation of the nation, or indeed replacing such a vision with the potentially more parochial concern of breeding the next generation.

Many Christians now and in Owen's day were baptised as babies but came to a living faith only later in life. It is perhaps natural for such people to question the validity of what could appear from their position of new-found vibrancy to have been merely an empty ritual. Yet just because a practice may have been abused in the past does not mean there is no right and proper, biblically-mandated use for it. For Owen to make it clear from the start that non-covenantal, indiscriminate baptism is not what paedobaptism is meant to be about could be incredibly helpful in preventing such people from (if I may put it like this) throwing out the baby of the biblical doctrine with the font water of nominal faith. We may be rightly skeptical about the policy of certain churches because they seem to have failed in their duty to preach the gospel clearly and nurture faith in those they initiate into baptism. Yet this should make us passionate not to abolish infant baptism but to see it reformed according to a more biblical pattern, administered and followed-up correctly. That, I believe, was Owen's concern in the face of radical antipaedobaptism in his day, when much that had been merely 'traditional' was reassessed and abandoned.

We must now turn to the substantive part of his argument to see if he was able to put the doctrine of infant

---

designation of choice in the title of his magnum opus) this is not meant as a slur, but merely as a convenient designation in this context.

[15] The theme of Owen's heart for gospel propagation is brought out in Toon, *God's Statesman* e.g. pages 41 and 80.

baptism on a sufficiently secure foundation to make its retention viable. We are dealing now, then, with the eight major sub-points of section IV.

## 2. Why not baptise infants?

Owen's first major point in effect throws back a question to those who would deny infant baptism. Where, he asks, does Scripture forbid such a thing? Which Bible text says that the children of believers should not be baptised? Opponents of infant baptism "can produce no testimony of Scripture wherein their negation is formally or in terms included, nor any one asserting what is inconsistent with the affirmative." That is, there is no verse forbidding infant baptism and no verse inconsistent with infant baptism. We have already noted above that some non-paedobaptists would point to a pattern in Acts where baptism follows the reception of preaching and a profession of faith. Tombes, for example, has a list of such verses, from which he logically concludes "in which places, profession of repentance and faith is still made the antecedent to baptism: but this does not agree to infants, therefore they are not to be baptised."[16] Yet Owen replies in a withering manner that, "it is weak beneath consideration to suppose that the requiring of the baptism of believers is inconsistent with that of their seed." That is, if one is going to oppose this practice, then one needs to produce clear arguments from Scripture which address it and oppose it directly. To assert that believers must be baptised is not a logical argument against baptising their

---

[16] Tombes, *Examen*, page 153 cf. Renihan, *Antipaedobaptism*, pages 132-135. As with all quotations made out of 17th century sources here, I have updated the spelling and punctuation. American readers will be delighted to learn that 'to baptise' and its cognates was often spelled with a 'z' in seventeenth century English. I have corrected this indelicacy.

children as well, since the two things are by no means mutually exclusive.

Owen's second major point is a similarly aggressive rhetorical thrust against what he perceives as the structural flaws in the antipaedobaptist case. Not only are there no verses against infant baptism, his opponents also have no examples in Scripture or in early church history where the children of believers were not given "the same sign and seal of the covenant" as their parents. There were no examples of circumcised fathers with uncircumcised sons or baptised parents with un-baptised children - if they were being brought up in the knowledge of God, then they received the same sign as their parents. There was no counterexample in Scripture or "the approved practice of the primitive church."[17] There was significant debate about the historical evidence from the early church,[18] but Owen's point is undeniable regarding the lack of evidence in Scripture. There were, Owen implies, serious and significant silences when it came to assessing the evidence for the non-paedobaptist case.

Owen was of course not alone in pointing to such gaps in the opposition's argument. Stephen Marshall had done the

[17] By which Owen means the early church of the first few centuries after Christ. See Renihan, *Antipaedobaptism*, page 145 where Tombes casts doubt on infant baptism in the early church saying, "it is a wonder to me, that if it were so manifest as you speak, you should find nothing in Eusebius for it, nor in Ignatius, nor in Clemens Alexandrinus, or in Athanasius, not in Epiphanius". Silences in historical remains could be taken either way it seems.

[18] One contemporary defence of a paedobaptist reading of the historical texts was Robert Ram's *Paedo-Baptisme or, The Baptising of Infants Justified* (London, 1645). The debate continued in the exchange between J. Jeremias, *Infant Baptism in the First Four Centuries* (London: SCM, 1960) and K. Aland, *Did the Early Church Baptize Infants?* (London: SCM, 1961).

same thing in his Westminster Abbey sermon which sparked off the initial publishing war with Anglican antipaedobaptist John Tombes. Like Owen, Marshall points out that nowhere in the New Testament is there a command "that the children of believers when they are grown, should be instructed and baptised, though instructed by their parents... nor any example where ever that was done." But he confessed that non-paedobaptists had their own spin regarding arguments from silence when they pointed out that "there is no command, no express institution, or clear example in all the New Testament of baptising of infants". To this he freely admitted, and yet he denied the legitimacy of the logical leap then made: to say "that Christians are not tied to observe that which is not expressly and in so many words set down in the New Testament" was "not true divinity". Why not? Because there were several areas in which Christians did not require a specific word in the New Testament to bind them: there was no express law against polygamy, for example, and no reiteration of the forbidden degrees of marriage (as in Leviticus 18).[19] Did that mean that Christians could take multiple wives or have sexual intercourse with their siblings? Surely not! There was no express command or example in the New Testament to justify women receiving the Lord's Supper either, but that did not mean they were not fit to partake of that sacrament. Should the children of believers be denied access to the other sacrament on the same grounds?[20]

Arguments from silence cannot be compelling on their own. They must be part of a larger case, as indeed they are for both Owen and Marshall. But it is significant that Owen begins here with a challenge to non-paedobaptists. It is common

[19] Though Marshall acknowledges Paul's horror regarding the specific incestuous relationship in 1 Corinthians 5.

[20] Marshall, *A Sermon of the Baptizing of Infants*, pages 34-35.

experience in many conservative evangelical circles today to find that the burden of proof on this issue is simply assumed to lie with paedobaptists. It is they who must justify what is sometimes considered to be their pragmatic continuance of a Roman Catholic practice, as if the case for not baptising infants was so patently obvious from Scripture as to not require justification.[21] Owen reminds us that there is a burden of proof on both sides of the divide here, and a heavy burden at that for antipaedobaptists. It is not an issue which can be easily and straightforwardly settled by brandishing a few proof-texts; it is more like trying to piece together a complex jigsaw in which some of the key pieces seem to be missing, and there is legitimate debate over how the gaps might be filled in a manner most in keeping with their surroundings.

So first, Owen challenges those against infant baptism to be more rigorous in their methodology and to admit the weaknesses in their case. Some of the pieces they would no doubt like to see are missing. Then once it is clear that this debate is not simply over the interpretation of a few isolated verses but over how the Bible as a whole is structured and put

---

[21] For a provocative exposure of and answer to this sort of thinking see P. J. Leithart's, "The Sociology of Infant Baptism" in *The Baptized Body* (Moscow, ID: Canon Press, 2007), pages 113-136 where he concludes (pages 135-136) that "Baptist theology and baptismal practice seem reasonable and natural only because our definitions of 'reasonable and natural' are thoroughly infected with the modern notion that consent is the alpha and omega of social, moral, and religious life." Indeed, early Anabaptists were committed theologically to 'free will' according to K. G. Miller, "Complex Innocence, Obligatory Nurturance, and Parental Vigilence: 'The Child' in the Work of Menno Simons" in Bunge, *The Child in Christian Thought*, page 207 and D. C. Steinmetz, *Luther in Context* (Bloomington: Indiana University Press, 1986), page 59 (on Hubmaier). More recently the case against paedobaptism has been argued differently, sometimes with more Reformed views of theological anthropology.

together it should be easier to proceed with a certain level of charity and patience born of humility. Inference and implication will have to play an important part in any answer to the question of infant baptism. So Owen will challenge us in subsequent arguments to recover confidence in a Reformed hermeneutic that sees the Bible as the one unfolding story of God's unchanging plan of salvation, a hermeneutic which provides the big picture into which infant baptism fits harmoniously, comfortably, and securely.

## 3. Making things worse for children

Owen's third major argument concerns the revocation of spiritual privileges given by God. The essence of his argument here is that if the non-paedobaptists are right, God has made things worse for the children of believers now that Christ has come. What he says is this: "A spiritual privilege once granted by God unto any cannot be changed, disannulled, or abrogated, without an especial divine revocation of it, or the substitution of a greater privilege and mercy in the room of it."

The spiritual privilege he refers to is that in Genesis 17 God granted the infant seed of believing Abraham a right to participate in the covenant, including its initial seal. The covenant was cut with Abraham and his children, and as part of it Abraham and his male children were all to receive the covenant sign.[22] To deny the children of believers that right to

---

[22] Owen does not make the rather obvious paedobaptist point here that Abraham (a 'believer' since at least Genesis 15:6) was definitely *not* told to wait until his children shared his faith before he circumcised them. Whilst it is true that it is those who believe who are sons of Abraham (Galatians 3:7) this cannot function as an argument against infant baptism since it evidently did not function as an argument against infant circumcision.

the initial seal of the covenant (though the sign may have been changed) cannot be appropriate unless God has expressly changed his instructions. As Marshall said in his sermon, speaking of the first disciples as they went about baptising and teaching, "it behoved the Lord to give them a caution for the leaving out of infants in this new administration, that they might know his mind, if that he intends to have them left out – which that ever he did in word or deed, cannot be found in the Scriptures."[23] Besides, God would only do that, Owen says, if he was replacing the privilege those children enjoyed with something greater for them, which antipaedobaptists do not think he has. Therefore, now that Christ has come, the children of believers are apparently in a worse situation spiritually than they were before, if the antipaedobaptists are correct.[24]

Owen traces out several implications of adopting this view. First, if the privilege given to the children of believers in Genesis 17 is now to be revoked, then the lordship of Christ over the church is being overruled. For he himself has not spoken to remove the right of children to receive the seal of the covenant, as Owen has already established: the New Testament says nothing about children now being excluded from the outward sign of covenant membership. So then, "To abolish or take away any grant of privilege made by him to the church, without his own express revocation of it, is to deny his sovereign authority."

---

[23] Marshall, *A Sermon of the Baptizing of Infants*, page 39.

[24] Antipaedobaptist Robert Barrow, *A Briefe Answer to A Discourse Lately Written by one P.B... Wherein is Declared... That the Baptizing of Infants hath no authority from the Scriptures* (London: 1642), page 13 declares simply that "although infants were of the church before Christ yet the Lord hath manifestly declared, that they should not be so now", basing his argument on Galatians 4:22-31.

Second, if a spiritual privilege given by God to his people is revoked then we should expect a greater privilege to have been granted in its place.[25] Otherwise it appears contrary to his goodness, love, and care for the church, which Owen does not wish to see impugned. It is one thing to remove, for example, the Jerusalem Temple and its glories but God clearly substituted in its place "a more glorious spiritual temple and worship" in Christ.

John Tombes had at least two answers to this sort of argument. First, he said that some individuals in the former dispensation did have greater privileges than those in the new; for example, "no man besides Abraham is called the father of the Faithful; no woman besides one, The mother of Christ".[26] This does not quite answer Owen here, since he clearly has in mind privileges of the covenant people in general, rather than individual privileges and blessings as part of salvation history.

Tombes's best answer to this type of argument was to throw back at paedobaptists what he saw as an inconsistency: if things cannot be worse for children under the new covenant then why not include infants in the Lord's Supper, since they were part of the Passover? He pointed to this inconsistency on many occasions.[27] Needless to say this aroused strong opposition from Marshall[28] and other puritans, who were not in favour of paedocommunion, partly on the grounds that whether

---

[25] Owen is not speaking here about the granting of spiritual gifts *to individuals*, which he may or may not decide to take away from time to time, as he wills.

[26] Renihan, *Antipaedobaptism*, page 125.

[27] See Renihan, *Antipaedobaptism*, page 123-124. A. H. Strong used this same argument in the 19th century and was answered by B. B. Warfield in "The Polemics of Infant Baptism" in *Studies in Theology, The Works of Benjamin B. Warfield: Volume 9* (Grand Rapids: Baker, reprinted 2003), pages 401-402.

[28] Marshall, *A Sermon of the Baptizing of Infants*, pages 51-52.

children participated in the Passover or not was a contentious point, and partly on the grounds that 1 Corinthians 11:28-29 seemed to them to lay down that participants should be capable of examining themselves spiritually and discerning the body, which infants could not.[29] Both the *Book of Common Prayer* and the *Westminster Directory of Public Worship* found no place for infants in the Lord's Supper, although it is now permitted and widely practiced in the Church of England, something which divides conservative evangelicals.[30] It may be that Jewett (no paedobaptist!) was right to say that, "the argument from the covenant for infant baptism, when managed with adroitness, has about it an aura of plausibility; but the more convincingly it is pressed, the more embarrassed is the defense [*sic*] of believer communion."[31]

Sadly, Owen does not address this tangential but significant question. He is, however, very concerned that if God were to make things worse for covenant children, to take away a spiritual privilege once solemnly granted, it would be particularly contrary to "his constant course of proceeding with it [the church] from the foundation of the world, wherein he

---

[29] Calvin had addressed the issue this way in *Institutes* 4.16.30. Some might argue on the basis of 1 Corinthians 10:1-5 that Paul envisages infants as being involved in both sacraments because they were involved in the Old Testament events Paul compares them to - baptism into Moses at the Red Sea, and partaking of the spiritual food of manna and water from the rock in the desert. I am grateful to Martin Foord for this insight.

[30] For discussion amongst conservative evangelical Anglicans on this issue, see R. Beckwith and A. Daunton-Fear, *The Water and the Wine: A Contribution to the Debate on Children and Holy Communion* (London: Latimer Trust, 2005) for an argument against paedocommunion, and M. Mason, "Covenant Children and Covenant Meals: Biblical Evidence for Infant Communion" in *Churchman* 121/2 (2007), pages 127-138 for an argument in favour.

[31] P. K. Jewett, *Infant Baptism and the Covenant of Grace* (Grand Rapids: Eerdmans, 1978), page 207.

went on in the enlargement and increase of its privileges until the coming of Christ." In other words, having a right to the seal of the covenant is a spiritual privilege, and things have always been improving and getting better for the church in terms of its spiritual privileges. There has been a progression in redemptive history. God's people were better off after Abraham than before; they were more blessed after Sinai, then with the replacement of the tabernacle for the more permanent Temple and its worship. The spiritual privileges of God's people were constantly being enlarged – with the grant of kingship, the sending of the prophets, and then with the coming of Christ and the Spirit. Owen's argument, then, is this: if this is how God works, why with the great and final revelation of his Son would he remove and revoke completely such an immense spiritual privilege as believers' children had previously enjoyed?[32]

---

[32] We might mention here the sometimes controversial question of how much the Old Testament saints knew about God. Even just a glance at volume 1 of his works shows that Owen is very clear on this. Speaking of the Old Testament and God revealing himself to Moses in Exodus 33:18-23 he says: "This is all that God would grant, viz., such external representations of himself, in the proclamation of his name, and created appearances of his glory, as we have of a man whose back parts only we behold as he passeth by us. But as to the being of God, and his subsistence in the Trinity of persons, we have no direct intuition into them, much less comprehension of them [that is, in the Old Testament]." See *Christologia: On the Person of Christ* in *The Works of John Owen: Volume 1* (Edinburgh: T&T Clark, 1862), page 67. Again, it is true of Old Testament saints that, "Neither they nor the angels knew clearly either the sufferings of Christ or the glory that should ensue." *Christologia*, page 263. And yet, "The meanest believer may now find out more of the work of Christ in the types of the Old Testament, than any prophets or wise men could have done of old." *Christologia*, page 101. This is because, "*when the Son of God 'appeared in the flesh,'* and in the discharge of his office, – God himself, as unto his being, and manner of existence in three distinct persons, with all the glorious properties of the divine nature, was illustriously manifested unto them that did believe" – *Meditations and*

To suppose that this is actually what God has done (which was the non-paedobaptist position) seemed to Owen to take away from the glory and honour of Christ and the gospel, the great culmination of all God's dealings with his people. He states that it would be contrary "to all his promises, the honour of Christ, and a multitude of express testimonies of Scripture." He does not at this stage cite which promises and Scriptures he has in mind, but Stephen Marshall's sermon cites Hebrews 8:6 and 2 Corinthians 3:10 amongst others as showing that the privileges of believers under the new covenant were greater, not less, than those under the old. He also points out that in Christ there is neither male nor female (Galatians 3:28) – so girls as well as boys may now be baptised, a clear enlargement of the privilege.[33] Tombes agreed that privileges had been enlarged, but only in regard to the inclusion of gentiles and the increased clarity of revelation in the new era.[34]

Later in his argument, however, Owen will refer to several Old Testament texts which mention believers and their children as *together* part of the future new order.[35] These texts certainly do not indicate that God will be going back on the inclusion of children within the covenant arrangement as soon as the messiah comes. So God has not left "the seed of believers, whilst in their infant state, in the same condition with those of pagans and infidels... contrary to God's covenant" as Owen accuses non-paedobaptists of believing. Quite the

---

*Discourses on the Glory of Christ* (also in volume 1), page 298 [emphasis mine].

[33] See Marshall, *A Sermon of the Baptizing of Infants*, page 30.

[34] Tombes, *Antipaedobaptism: Part 3*, pages 704-705.

[35] He refers to Isaiah 22:24, 44:3, 61:9, and 65:23. We might also add the 'everlasting' covenant prophecies such as Isaiah 59:20-21, Jeremiah 32:38-40, or Ezekiel 37:25.

contrary, God's promises assure believers about the continuing status and importance of their children in God's plan.[36]

There is a powerful pastoral argument here which all those tasked with the spiritual education of children would do well to ponder. Should we think of them as "pagans and infidels" requiring evangelisation, which Owen points out is the logical conclusion of seeing believers' children as outside the covenant?[37] It is of course agreed by people on both sides of the debate that "we as Christians should give ourselves to teaching the gospel to our children and praying for them privately and publicly" and that "children of believing parents do not need baptism to be taught the Ten Commandments, the Lord's Prayer, and the gospel in all its fullness." Paedobaptists and non-paedobaptists can both pray "that none of our children ever know any lengthy period of conscious rebellion against God".[38] Yet the antipaedobaptist position requires a fundamentally different attitude to be adopted towards such children.

For instance, Mark Dever insists that Christians should "not treat your children as if you presume they are elect" and "parents should not presume to be certain of their children's

---

[36] See also Owen's comments on Hebrews 4:15 in Goold (ed.), *The Works of John Owen: Volume 21* (Volume 20 in the Banner of Truth edition, i.e. volume 4 of the Hebrews commentary), pages 417-418 which are on these same lines.

[37] Peter Leithart, *The Baptised Body*, page 115, speaks in a similar way to Owen about the Baptist view of children: "The nurture of their early years may indeed involve Christian training – instruction in the Bible, teaching the child to pray, involvement in the church, and so forth – but it is not seen as the nurture of a *Christian* child... it is nurture of a pagan or unbelieving or neutral child."

[38] Mark Dever, "Baptism in the Context of the Local Church" in *Believer's Baptism*, pages 333, 350, and 348 footnote 28.

faith."[39] So must they be taught that passages such as Ephesians 1:1-14 are inapplicable to them personally, since they are only allowed to look in at the blessings of the predestined Christian objectively, from the outside? And would it not be inconsistent for children presumed to be un-elect and without faith to be permitted to sing, for example, the verse from "In Christ Alone" with which this study began, since it puts into their mouths such confident assertions about their eternal security? Other Reformed Baptists would agree that it is presumptuous to nurture our children as if they could be disciples of Christ without a conversion experience or at least mature intellectual capacity.[40] So it seems that although they *may* be converted before they are permitted to drive a car, we must not speak to our children in a way that implies we think they have been, but should instead wait and see how they turn out later.[41]

On the other hand, passages such as Ephesians 6:1-4 do seem to call on Christian parents to treat their children *as Christians*. From their earliest years they are not just to be 'taught about God' but nurtured within the covenant and disciplined according to it (verse 4). In verses 1-3 children are even commanded to obey their parents "in the Lord" (ἐν κυρίῳ, *en kurio*) and are given a promise to be apprehended by faith. Interestingly, they are not commanded here to repent and believe "just like mummy and daddy did", but to grow in the family faith as they are nurtured in obedience to it. Presumably

---

[39] "Baptism in the Context of the Local Church", page 343 footnote 17 (sub-point 17) and page 349.

[40] See e.g. D. Grundersen, *Your Child's Profession of Faith* (Amityville, NY: Calvary Press, 1994). For a critical paedobaptist review of this, see R. Lusk, *Paedofaith: A Primer on the Mystery of Infant Salvation and a Handbook for Covenant Parents* (Monroe, LA: Athanasius Press, 2005), pages 154-158.

[41] "'Time will tell' is the point of many of Christ's parables" says Dever, page 333.

if Paul can apply the command and promise of the fifth commandment to the children of believers in Ephesus then some other appropriate scriptural (covenantal) promises, threats, comforts, and assurances might also be held out to them to receive and accept by faith.

In Ephesians 6, Paul chose to emphasise the positive side of the fifth commandment rather than speaking about the sanction children could face if they broke it under the old covenant (e.g. Deuteronomy 21:18-21). Such positive motivations can work exceptionally well, so that we do not need to indulge in "frightening poor innocent children with talk of hell fire and eternal damnation" as some might, in order to somehow provoke a conversion experience.[42] As Lewis Schenck rightly says, "It was unfortunate that the Great Awakening made an emotional experience, involving terror, misery, and depression, the only approach to God."[43] Some may never have such an experience, but grow up knowing and loving Jesus from their earliest days. At some point they will be born again, but it may be an unnoticed, un-dramatic event. Would it be right to presume such children are unregenerate and un-elect?

Moreover, a child's faith may not have the cognitive sophistication of an adult's, but that does not mean they are incapable of relying on and trusting Christ until they have

---

[42] The great American preacher Jonathan Edwards was accused of this, with some justification it seems, according to Brekus, "Children of Wrath, Children of Grace", page 321 (see also pages 313-320 on his sermons to children). See the careful remarks of T. A. Sizemore, *Of Such is the Kingdom: Nurturing Children in the Light of Scripture* (Fearn, Ross-Shire: Christian Focus, 2000), page 67 on Edwards and his context.
[43] L. B. Schenck, *The Presbyterian Doctrine of Children in the Covenant: An Historical Study of the Significance of Infant Baptism in the Presbyterian Church* (Phillipsburg, NJ: P&R, [1940] 2003), page 71.

passed through puberty.[44] Nor does it suggest that all we can do is teach them 'law' (to be nice, obedient sinners) until they are old enough to 'grasp the gospel properly' and be saved. Speaking of infants, Jesus said that "of such is the kingdom of heaven" (Matthew 19:14). He did not just mean that people who are like children in some way are saved, (a point made elsewhere in Matthew 18:3)[45] but that infants themselves would make up a part of his kingdom.[46] Yet as Owen argues it, to see

---

[44] Jewett, *Infant Baptism and the Covenant of Grace*, page 168 is right to say that "few have found the courage to rest the weight of their case on so tenuous a foundation" as the idea that very young babies have "a kind of inchoate faith germinating like a seed in the soul". Some like Lusk, *Paedofaith* would build a great deal on the idea of 'baby faith' (from Psalm 22:9-10 for example), and it is true that Luther, Calvin, and Turretin spoke about a kind of faith in infants. But the case for infant baptism does not need to include or rest upon this, as P. C. Marcel, *The Biblical Doctrine of Infant Baptism: Sacrament of the Covenant of Grace* trans. P. E. Hughes (London: James Clarke, 1953), pages 209-218 clearly shows.

[45] The word is τοιούτων (*toiouton*, 'of such') in the Greek of Matthew 19:14, Mark 10:14 and Luke 18:16. Bearing in mind how this adjective is used elsewhere in the Gospels (e.g. Matthew 9:8; Mark 4:33, 6:2, 7:13; Luke 9:9; John 4:23), it simply cannot mean "those *like* this" while excluding the children themselves. See also Calvin's comments on Matthew 19:14 in *Commentary on a Harmony of the Evangelists*, Calvin's Commentaries Volume XVI (Grand Rapids: Baker, 1993), pages 390-391 (volume 2) and the comments of Spurgeon (a Baptist) quoted in Sizemore, *Of Such is the Kingdom*, page 136.

[46] Charles Hodge, *Systematic Theology: Volume 1* (Hendrickson, reprinted 1999), page 27 says, "Of such He tells us is the kingdom of heaven, as though heaven was, in great measure, composed of the souls of redeemed infants". See also the similar thoughts of J. C. Ryle, *Expository Thoughts on Luke: Volume 2* (Edinburgh: Banner of Truth, 1986), page 268 on Luke 18:16. Though it must be noted, as Ryle says in *Expository Thoughts on Mark* (Edinburgh: Banner of Truth, 1985), page 203, "Of course, it is not pretended that there is any mention of baptism, or even any reference to it in [Mark 10:13-16]. All we mean to say is that

the children of believers as "young servants of the king"[47] is compatible and consistent only with the paedobaptist position. Since they have that immense privilege, however, the church has a duty towards children: to pray for them, to instruct them "according unto their capacities", to advise parents on their upbringing, to visit and encourage them, and to prepare them to come into "full communion" with the church. Owen therefore advised that not only should parents be taught about their duties and responsibilities towards their children, but each church should have a teacher set aside especially for their instruction.[48]

## 4. Infant regeneration and salvation

Someone may ask, 'Granted that children may be regenerate (God does not work in adults alone), does that necessarily mean they ought to be baptised?' As a Baptist, for instance, Mark Dever states that "refusal to baptize is not intended as a statement asserting that the child is not regenerate but simply as a reluctance publicly to affirm that which has not yet been maturely evidenced."[49] Obviously this line of argument contains something of a Baptistic presupposition that baptism is about affirming the candidate's faith, whereas Reformed paedobaptists like Owen would be happier to say that it was primarily about

the expressions and gestures of our Lord in this passage, are a *strong indirect argument* in favour of infant baptism" (emphasis mine).

[47] R. C. Sproul, "In Jesus' Name, Amen" in G. Strawbridge (ed.), *The Case for Covenantal Infant Baptism* (Phillipsburg, NJ: P&R, 2003), page 310.

[48] *The True Nature of a Gospel Church*, pages 22-24 in *The Works of John Owen: Volume 16*.

[49] "Baptism in the Context of the Local Church", page 350. The context is more about young children who profess belief than infants who have just been born, but the point is the same.

the promise and covenant of God.[50] Yet even if such an argument could be made without this presupposition, Owen will not accept the core idea that someone can be regenerate and yet denied a right to baptism. The two things go together – "They that have the thing signified have a right unto the sign of it". This is the core of Owen's fourth and fifth points in section IV.

The text which undergirds Owen's argument here is Acts 10:47. There we find the apostle Peter and his believing Jewish colleagues amazed at the grace of God shown to the gentiles gathered at Cornelius's house. When they received the Holy Spirit, Peter asked, "Can anyone withhold water for baptizing these people, who have received the Holy Spirit just as we have?" Owen takes this as a principle, that those who are partakers in the thing signified have a right to the outward sign of it. How can they be denied the lesser if they already possess the greater? Later he cites Acts 2:38-39 as also demonstrating this same principle, and says, "That unto whom the covenant or promise doth belong, to them belongs the administration of the initial seal of it." Interestingly, the Ethiopian Eunuch in Acts 8:36 asks, "What prevents me from being baptised?" which also appears to be consistent with this way of thinking: he believed the good news brought to him by Philip and wondered if there was any reason why he should not therefore receive the sign of baptism. Philip's consequent baptising of him would seem to demonstrate early agreement with this principle.[51]

---

[50] Miller, "Complex Innocence", page 201 avers that "For Simons, baptism represents the believer's faith, while for Luther and Calvin baptism represents God's promise, a contrast Simons may not fully grasp or appreciate." Not all Baptists would agree with Menno Simons or Mark Dever of course!

[51] It should be noted that whereas some Baptist exegesis of Acts assumes that the pattern of 'faith then baptism' seen there must be normative for today, Dever and others must argue that the equally prevalent pattern of

Owen then considers the application of this principle to children. He states that the children of believers are all capable of the grace signified in baptism. That is, they are not angels or animals incapable of regeneration but have the potential to be born again.[52] But then he moves into what might today be considered much more controversial territory when he says that some of those children "are certainly partakers of [that grace], namely, such as die in their infancy... therefore they may and ought to be baptised". Owen assumes that the children of believers who die in infancy are partakers of the grace signified in baptism – that is, regeneration, new birth – just as much as those who profess faith as adults are. And he concludes that since that is the case, they ought to be baptised. He is not arguing for the post-mortem baptism of dead children.[53] He is arguing that since believers' children are capable of the grace signified (as evidenced in the salvation of those who die in infancy) they ought to be permitted the sign.[54]

---

immediate baptism after conversion "need not be the normative practice today" ("Baptism in the Context of the Local Church" page 334 footnote 11).

[52] They also have *potentia credendi*, the potential to believe, though as with adults the transformation of this into an actual disposition of faith must be a gracious gift of God (see Philippians 1:29; 2 Peter 1:1,3; Ephesians 2:8). God is free to give this to whoever he chooses; a mature intellectual capacity is never made a pre-condition for his gift. Infant salvation, therefore, does not entail a denial of salvation by faith alone – unless faith is thought to be a 'work' which only adults are capable of performing, rather than a gift granted by God to his elect (see Acts 13:48).

[53] This is not his solution to the debate over the meaning of 'baptism for the dead' in 1 Corinthians 15:29!

[54] J. C. Ryle, *Expository Thoughts on Mark* (Edinburgh: Banner of Truth, 1985), page 204 argues in the same vein in comments on Mark 10:16, saying, "It is allowed on all sides that infants may be elect and chosen of God unto salvation – may be washed in Christ's blood, born again of the Spirit, have grace, be justified, sanctified, and enter heaven. If these

How can Owen base so much on infant regeneration and salvation? It helps to understand that this was not a widely disputed point in his day. Broadly speaking, most Reformed theologians around Owen's time agreed that the infants of believers, dying in infancy, were saved.[55] As Lewis Schenck says, "The Reformed church has always believed, on the basis of God's immutable promise, that all children of believers dying in infancy were saved... because the promise was 'unto us and our children.'"[56] Kuyper adds an important qualifier here when he says that Calvinists "have never usurped the right to pronounce on the presence or absence of spiritual life in infants. They only stated how God would have us *consider* such infants, and this consideration based on the divine word made it imperative to look upon their infant children as elect and saved, and to treat them accordingly."[57]

There were, however, some differences of opinion in the Reformed tradition regarding the children of unbelievers. Some, such as Zwingli, Bishop John Hooper, and Augustus Montague Toplady saw death in infancy as a sign of God's election, whoever the child's parents were. Others rejected the idea that any infant dying outside the covenant was saved. Many, like the great puritan Bible commentator Matthew Henry, were merely agnostic about those born to unbelievers. Owen's own view is that since God is perfectly free to elect

---

things be so, it is hard to see why they may not receive the outward sign of baptism".

[55] B. B. Warfield, "The Development of the Doctrine of Infant Salvation" in *Studies in Theology, The Works of Benjamin B. Warfield: Volume 9*, pages 429-438.

[56] Schenck, *The Presbyterian Doctrine of Children in the Covenant*, page 118. See Calvin, Institutes, 4.16.17-19.

[57] Quoted in Schenck, *The Presbyterian Doctrine*, page 18. See also the views of Richard Baxter, which accord with this, in *The Nonconformist Advocate* (1679), page 53 (Part 2).

anyone there may well be some infants born and dying outside the covenant who are nevertheless saved: he had "no doubt but that God taketh many unto him in Christ whose parents never knew, or had been despisers of, the gospel."[58] Yet when it came to the children of believers there was a great consensus that (as the Synod of Dort puts it), "godly parents ought not to doubt of the election and salvation of their children whom God calls out of this life in their infancy".[59]

Owen, therefore, seems to be building on an essentially undisputed truth and trying to establish another "by good and necessary consequence" (as *Westminster Confession* 1.6 says). Marshall had also done something similar in his sermon.[60] Such an appeal was possible because even many non-paedobaptists believed firmly in the salvation of those who die in infancy. The view of 16th century Anabaptist leader Menno Simons may in fact have been closest to Zwingli's position,[61] as

---

[58] *Display of Arminianism* (1642) in *The Works of John Owen: Volume 10*, page 81. I can find no basis for saying that Owen believes that all who die in infancy are elect as is claimed in T. L. Tiessen, *Who Can Be Saved? Reassessing Salvation in Christ and World Religions* (Leicester: IVP, 2004), page 210 (citing A. H. Strong), though this is one of the most insignificant of the inadequacies in Tiessen's analysis. I am deeply unconvinced by the analogy he draws between saved infants and unevangelized adults, and unimpressed by the atomistic exegesis he uses to defend it and undermine alternatives.

[59] Article 1.17 in *The Judgement Of The Synode Holden at Dort* (London: John Bill, 1619). The 1662 *Book of Common Prayer* declares that, "It is certain by God's Word, that children which are baptised, dying before they commit actual sin, are undoubtedly saved." See L. Gatiss, *The Tragedy of 1662: The Ejection and Persecution of the Puritans* (London: Latimer Trust, 2007), pages 22-23 for some puritan objections to this.

[60] Marshall, *A Sermon of the Baptizing of Infants*, page 45.

[61] See Miller, "Complex Innocence", page 203.

was that of 19th century Baptist Charles Haddon Spurgeon.[62] This may not be entirely consistent[63] and Tombes, it should be said, was much less certain about infant salvation.[64]

Owen does not here elaborate on all the details of the doctrine itself,[65] though it is important to note that he does not

---

[62] In I. H. Murray (ed.), *Letters of Charles Haddon Spurgeon*, (Edinburgh: Banner of Truth, 1992), page 150 (Letter 1869), Spurgeon says, "I have never, at any time in my life, said, believed, or imagined that any infant, under any circumstances, would be cast into hell. I have always believed in the salvation of all infants... I do not believe that, on this earth, there is a single professing Christian holding the damnation of infants; or, if there be, he must be insane; or utterly ignorant of Christianity." His Sermon number 411 "Infant Salvation" (available at http://www.spurgeon.org/sermons/0411.htm) is equally emotive, "If we had a God, whose name was Moloch, if God were an arbitrary tyrant, without benevolence or grace, we could suppose some infants being cast into hell; but our God, who heareth the young ravens when they cry, certainly will find no delight in the shrieks and cries of infants cast away from his presence."

[63] In his sermon (page 45), Marshall points out that if (on antipaedobaptist assumptions) faith *must* precede baptism for children as well as adults because Scripture says faith is essential for salvation, then that precludes infants from being saved not just from being baptised. Marcel, *The Biblical Doctrine of Infant Baptism*, pages 213-214 makes the same point.

[64] Although he says in *Antipaedobaptism: Part 3* that "salvation belongs to some infants" (page 562) and "there is ground for a strong hope of the salvation of infants of Christian believers so dying" (page 557), even a "strong probability" (page 560), his overall conclusion is that "there is no certainty concerning the salvation of this or that particular infant of a believer dying, nor is there a sure ground for faith concerning it, nor is the hope of it certain, and we are to suspend our judgement concerning it" (page 555).

[65] For more on this, see R. H. Nash, *When a Baby Dies: Answers to Comfort Grieving Parents* (Grand Rapids: Zondervan, 1999) and R. A. Webb, *The Theology of Infant Salvation* (Harrisonburg, Virginia: Sprinkle Publications, [1907] 2003). Owen would no doubt approve of the insistence by Nash, Webb, and Warfield that confidence in infant salvation is only coherent if one has a Calvinist (monergistic) soteriology,

affirm that infants are 'innocent' or worthy of salvation: he is quite clear that they are born in sin (Psalm 51:5), spiritually dead, and facing God's curse (Ephesians 2:1-3).[66] So, he says, the only way they can be saved is if they are regenerated, born again (John 3:3).[67] He could point to 2 Samuel 12:22-23 as an example of an infant being saved,[68] and Luke 1:15 as an example of an infant (even an embryo) being filled with the Spirit.[69] This is far from proving the salvation or regeneration of every infant of course; yet it does demonstrate that a mature capacity to understand the gospel is not strictly necessary, biblically speaking, for infants to be regenerate or saved. So we cannot infer that they are automatically damned on the basis of original

---

and is not strictly possible in a consistently Arminian or semi-Pelagian theology.

[66] It is important to stress that we are here discussing infants who die in infancy, not all infants. Some infants grow up to reject the gospel, and no-one would say they were saved simply by virtue of having once been infants!

[67] As a contrast to this, and to attempts to root infant salvation in election, see the view of W. H. Griffith-Thomas in A. H. Hamilton, "The Doctrine of Infant Salvation: Part 2" in *BSac* 101/404 (October 1944), 472-473, who bases it upon a supposed universality in the atonement. The same link can be found in a seventeenth century funeral sermon for an infant by Samuel Acton, *Dying Infants Sav'd by Grace, Proved* (London: 1699), page 9. See Warfield's answer to this contention in "The Doctrine of Infant Salvation", page 439.

[68] Owen alludes to this text in his letter to Lady Hartopp, on the death of her daughter (see appendix 2). He is equally clear that the child's enjoyment of blessedness is a result of God's grace alone, shown in his covenant promises. Tombes denies this exegesis of the text in *Antipaedobaptism: Part 3*, page 558.

[69] Cf. Luke 1:41, 66. Some have also seen 2 Kings 4:8-37, Job 3:16-17, Ecclesiastes 6:3-6 and Jeremiah 31:15-17 (cf. Matthew 2:18) as important texts to consider here.

sin or because they are unable to access the means of grace.[70] Owen's conclusion is that "regeneration is the grace whereof baptism is a sign or token. Wherever this is, there baptism ought to be administered.... infants who die in their infancy have the grace of regeneration, and consequently as good a right unto baptism as believers themselves."

In his fifth point, Owen makes the case that if God explicitly does not want someone to be baptised then they are eternally damned, since the sign and the grace must go together. This is why impenitent sinners are not to be baptised, because not having the reality they have no right to the sign. But he goes on to say that if the sign is denied to believers' infants then that implies (by the same logic) that God is denying them the reality of salvation too – "and then all the children of believing parents dying in infancy must, without hope, be eternally damned". He does not wish to contemplate such a consequence. It is certainly not that for Owen baptism is essential for salvation, but rather that if God desires the sign of salvation to be withheld it must be because he withholds salvation itself from such infants.[71]

What shall we make of Owen's attempt to use infant regeneration/salvation as part of his case for infant baptism? As

---

[70] *Westminster Confession* 10.3 (Savoy 10.3) says that "Elect infants, dying in infancy, are regenerated, and saved by Christ, through the Spirit, who worketh when, and where, and how he pleaseth: so also are all other elect persons who are incapable of being outwardly called by the ministry of the Word."

[71] Owen says elsewhere that elect infants are saved even if they die before being baptised. See *A Discourse of Spiritual Gifts*, page 432 of *The Works of John Owen: Volume 4*. W. Hubbock, *An Apologie of Infants in a Sermon: Proving by the revealed will of God that children prevented by death of their baptisme, by Gods election, may be saved* (London: 1595), page 9 takes issue especially with the Roman Catholic view that infants dying before baptism are damned.

a recognition that baptism and the language of regeneration often go together in Scripture (e.g. Galatians 3:26-27, Romans 6:3-4), it could be helpful. As an argument for the baptism of anyone who is regenerate, it has obvious strengths. As an argument for the baptism of those infants of believers who are about to die it has some coherence, if one grants the idea that such infants are saved. However, if Owen is arguing for more (i.e. that all believers' children should be baptised), there seems to be a gap in his logic here, a missing step. Such an argument may be represented like this:

1. Believers' infants are capable of being regenerated (of which baptism is the sign).
2. Some of them definitely are regenerated (i.e. those who die in infancy).
3. Therefore believers' infants should be baptised.

Step 3 does not seem to be a legitimate conclusion, given his premises. What is being left unsaid here? Is he suggesting, as some do, that we presume all believers' infants are in some sense regenerate and therefore have a right to be baptised?[72] If so, he leaves the 'presumed regeneration' step in the argument un-stated. Or is he merely talking about the capacity to be regenerate? If so, he has left himself open to the suggestion that on his logic anyone who is *capable* of being regenerated should be baptised. And does that not include the children of

[72] See Schenck, *The Presbyterian Doctrine*, pages xiv, 11. For an overview of Reformed debates over presumptive regeneration and whether it can be used as a basis for infant baptism, see R. J. Mouw, "Baptism and the Salvific Status of Children: An Examination of Some Intra-Reformed Debates" in *CTJ 41* (2006), pages 242-251. G. Vos, *Redemptive History and Biblical Interpretation* (Phillipsburg, NJ: P&R, 1980), page 264 points out that many Reformed theologians (including Ursinus, Voetius, and Witsius) use an argument from the regeneration of covenant children who die in infancy in their polemics with Anabaptists.

unbelievers, since he himself held that some of them are undoubtedly elect and so will be regenerated at some point? Yet he has already stated that such should not be baptised.

Has he therefore proved too much with this argument? The solution here does not appear to be straightforward or clearly spelled out in the condensed line of reasoning Owen presents. I do not think he is merely trying to establish that we should baptise all believers' children *in case* they die and prove thereby to have had a right to baptism (because, dying in infancy, they are saved). The evidence Owen brings can, however, be successfully deployed against his opponents' presuppositions in this way: if some children are saved they must be regenerated, and if regenerated then they have a theological right to be baptised; and if at least *some* children have a legitimate right to be baptised, then antipaedobaptists are wrong to say that no child should be baptised.[73]

Certainly to read Owen this way fits his polemical context and makes good logical sense of his otherwise difficult argument. On this reading, it does present a substantial counter to a familiar non-paedobaptist assertion, building on a commonly agreed premise that would be hard (theologically and pastorally) to deny. Yet however we evaluate the success or otherwise of this particular line of reasoning, clearly this argument involving the undeveloped assumption of infant salvation is not sufficient to establish the validity of infant baptism on its own.

## 5. Children and parents go together

The principle that the sign (the external rite) and the grace (the spiritual reality) of baptism go together may be on firmer

---

[73] I am grateful to Gert van den Brink for pointing me to this solution.

ground in Owen's sixth sub-point. Here he contends that children are by nature part of the same covenant as their parents, and are said by Scripture to be associated in it with them.[74] If true, this would be a strong argument that the sign of the covenant ought to be administered to them, since they already possess the covenant relationship which it seals. This perspective conceives of 'the thing signified' by baptism as at least partly a covenant relationship which can be objectively verified rather than an inner spiritual reality (such as regeneration) which cannot. Hence Owen argues from creation and from Romans 5:14 and 1 Corinthians 7:14 that children are dealt with by God in terms of the same covenant as their parents and "those who, by God's appointment, and by virtue of the law of their creation, are, and must of necessity be, included in the covenant of their parents, have the same right with them unto the privileges of that covenant."

This argument is more in keeping with the general thrust of his argument in previous points about the covenant. It argues on the basis of objective covenantal categories rather than from presumed or inferred subjective spiritual realities in the child itself, and is thus able to be focused on a promise of God which is where the Reformed doctrine is always strong. Stephen Marshall had used a similar line of defence, saying "Thus it is by the laws of almost all nations... children follow the covenant-condition of their parents."[75] Whether 1 Corinthians 7:14 could be used to prove the "federal holiness" of the children of believers was of course hotly disputed. Marshall defended against several objections but Tombes summarised the usual rejoinder when he pointed out that on Marshall's exegesis of the passage an unbelieving spouse could legitimately be said to be

[74] See also his comments on Hebrews 9:18-22 in *The Works of John Owen: Volume 23* (Volume 6 of Hebrews), page 354.

[75] Marshall, *A Sermon of the Baptizing of Infants*, page 15.

part of the covenant and therefore be baptised, just as much as the children of such a union, since both were said to be "holy".[76]

Marshall and Tombes argued over whether 1 Corinthians 7:14 was referring to matrimonial/civil legitimacy or federal holiness/status.[77] Either way, however, Owen is not using the verse to say children are holy and therefore should be baptised, as some would.[78] He is merely using it as an example of how children are accounted to be in the same covenantal state as their parents. Whether the status being referred to is civil or spiritual, the verse does clearly show that the children share that legal standing with their parents, which is all Owen is asking it to prove. If children share the same legal standing within the covenant as their parents then they have a right to the sign and seal of that covenant.

For all its strengths, this argument must also account somehow for the strand of biblical evidence which does see baptism specifically as a sign of regeneration / new life and not merely a covenant relationship e.g. Romans 6:3-4 and Colossians 2:11-12. The Anglican answer is to say that "Baptism is not only a sign of profession, and mark of difference, whereby Christian men are discerned from others that be not christened, but it is also a sign of Regeneration or New-Birth, whereby, as by an instrument, they that receive Baptism rightly are grafted into the Church" (Article 27). The right reception or efficacious appropriation of baptism may occur in or some time after the sign itself is applied. It is of course the response of faith, which

---

[76] Tombes, *An Examen*, page 79. Marshall in turn responded with further exegesis in *A Defence of Infant-Baptism* (London, 1646), pages 145-164.

[77] W. Hubbock, *An Apologie of Infants*, page 22 referred to the view Tombes espoused as a Jesuit argument!

[78] *A Directory For The Publique Worship of God* (London, 1645) otherwise known as the *Westminster Directory*, states (page 21) that those baptised "are Christians, and fœderally holy before baptism, and therefore are they baptised."

enjoys the benefits granted by the legal 'instrument' of baptism.[79] Owen would agree elsewhere that baptism is linked to the new life spoken of in Romans 6, and is clear that without eventual faith all the privileges and benefits of baptism are lost.[80]

Again we see then that the case for infant baptism has to be made by way of inference, consequence, and careful deduction. It cannot be decided simply by way of decisive proof-texting. Owen, however, is on clearer ground when he returns to arguments concerned with the covenant, and his logic here is less confusing than in the previous point.

## 6. Final arguments

Owen's seventh argument revolves again around the covenant which God made with Abraham to be God to him and to his offspring. Elsewhere he argues that whenever God declares that he will be God to someone ("I will be your God...") this is covenant language, by which God engages himself to work on

---

[79] The famous Gorham Judgment delivered by the supreme tribunal of the Church of England in 1850 found that, "the grace of regeneration does not so necessarily accompany the act of baptism that regeneration invariably takes place in baptism; that the grace may be granted before, in, or after baptism; that baptism is an effectual sign of grace by which God works invisibly in us, but only in such as worthily receive it – in them alone it has a wholesome effect; and that without reference to the qualification of the recipient it is not in itself an effectual sign of grace; that infants baptized and dying before actual sin are undoubtedly saved, but that in no case is baptism unconditional." See J. R. W. Stott, "The Evangelical Doctrine of Baptism" in *Churchman* 112/1 (1998), page 54. *Westminster Confession* 28.6 (Savoy 29.6) also states that, "The efficacy of baptism is not tied to that moment of time wherein it is administered".

[80] See *A Discourse Concerning the Holy Spirit,* pages 560-561 in *The Works of John Owen: Volume 3* and *The True Nature of a Gospel Church,* page 12 (Volume 16).

their behalf and for their good.[81] So if God promises to be God to the children of believers, he is taking them into covenant with himself. This is what he explicitly said to Abraham in Genesis 17:7, declares Owen, and Christ has fulfilled that very same covenant: he came to "confirm the promises given to the patriarchs" (Romans 15:8), and to be "the messenger of the covenant" (Malachi 3:1).[82] So, he argues, if God is no longer a God unto believers *and their offspring*, if believers' children are no longer to be part of the covenant, then Christ has not faithfully confirmed the truth of God in his promise to Abraham. We can no longer trust God to keep his promises! To get around this, Tombes wanted to deny that the covenant of which Christ was the messenger was the same as the Abrahamic covenant; that was "not a pure Gospel-covenant" but "mixed" he claimed, with some spiritual, some temporal and material promises.[83] Owen, however, replies that, "Let it be named what covenant he was the messenger of, if not of this. Occasional additions of temporal promises do not in the least alter the nature of the covenant."

According to Owen, Christ has fulfilled "the covenant with Abraham, enlarged and explained by following promises." Not only did the original promise include Abraham's children but Owen goes on to list other verses where it is said that "the promises made unto the fathers were, that their infant seed, their buds and offspring, should have an equal share in the

---

[81] *The Works of John Owen: Volume 19* (Hebrews, volume 2), page 84. The context is a discussion of the *pactum salutis* or covenant of redemption, whereby the Father and the Son covenanted together in eternity concerning our salvation. I am grateful to Professor Willem van Asselt for pointing me to Owen's exegetical argument here.

[82] Owen also cites Luke 1:72-73 as showing that Christ's coming was explicitly related to God remembering "his holy covenant, the oath he swore to our father Abraham".

[83] Renihan, *Antipaedobaptism*, page 72.

covenant with them" (Isaiah 22:24, 44:3, 61:9, 65:23). So again, to deny that children of believing parents had the same right and interest in the covenant as their parents was "plainly to deny the fidelity of Christ in the discharge of his office." If children are not to be accounted a part of the same covenant as their believing parents then Jesus has not done what he promised he would do, and God cannot be trusted. This again is a variant on the covenant arguments that Owen has already presented, but proven from different texts. Importantly, he makes it clear that children were included in God's plans long before the 'old covenant' of Sinai ("the covenant in its legal administration"). Their inclusion predates the now abolished Mosaic law but was part of the more comprehensive and overarching covenant promise to Abraham which endures in Christ.

We are ready now to hear his summary of the case:

> In brief, a participation of the seal of the covenant is a spiritual blessing. This the seed of believers was once solemnly invested in by God himself. This privilege he hath nowhere revoked, though he hath changed the outward sign; nor hath he granted unto our children any privilege or mercy in lieu of it now under the gospel, when all grace and privileges are enlarged to the utmost. His covenant promises concerning them, which are multiplied, were confirmed by Christ as a true messenger and minister; he gives the grace of baptism unto many of them, especially those that die in their infancy, owns children to belong unto his kingdom, esteems them disciples, appoints households to be baptized without exception. And who shall now rise up, and withhold water from them?

Owen adds here the argument often made from the household baptisms in Acts,[84] as part of the overall picture being developed. Like Warfield, he does realise that "infant baptism should not be founded solely on these passages alone",[85] yet they do provide potential evidence at least that where there were children present (other baptisms in Acts were of solitary individuals or groups of adults) they were included in the administration of the seal of the covenant for "the culture of that day assumed that children were usually part of the family... the preference is for, not against, the inclusion of family members. It had been that way since the time of Noah (Genesis 7:1), Abraham (Genesis 17:12-13), Joshua (Joshua 24:15), and David (2 Samuel 12:10)."[86]

Owen's eighth and last point is to say that more could be said, and arguments from church history could usefully be employed at this stage of the argument. Indeed, he goes on to engage in just such an argument (against Mr. Tombes) on the very next page. It may well be significant that since his brief opening remarks about the silences of church history, he has only put forward biblical and doctrinal evidence, choosing to consign further arguments over church history to the end of the case (and not really developing them to any great extent). It is possible that this could be construed as something of a rebuke or correction to Tombes, Marshall, and others who indulged in extensive historical arguments at the beginning of their works on the subject, prior to biblical exegesis. Whether such a rebuke is intended here, it is certainly safe to say that for Owen we should begin with the Bible and build our doctrine from there.

---

[84] Acts 16:15, 16:32-33, 18:8. See also Acts 11:14 and 1 Corinthians 1:16. Marshall also enlists the household baptisms in a minor role in his *Sermon of the Baptizing of Infants*, page 40.

[85] Warfield, "The Polemics of Infant Baptism", page 397. Stein, "Baptism in Luke-Acts", page 62 warns against building too much on them.

[86] J. M. Watt, "The *Oikos* Formula" in Strawbridge, *The Case for Covenantal Infant Baptism*, page 84.

Church history and custom is important but should never be primary when it comes to determining our present practice.

## Conclusion

Owen presents a rationale for covenantal infant baptism. He defines the question carefully, and sets about proving his case with biblical and theological arguments designed to interact with and counter the attack made on the practice by antipaedobaptists such as John Tombes.[87] He has his eye throughout on the glory and honour of Christ which he perceives to be under threat if the children of believers are not given the sign of the covenant which Christ has confirmed. He seeks to defend not just a doctrine but the loving care God has for the church, which he felt was not always adequately appreciated. He argues by way of inference and consequence, sometimes less successfully, but always with a view to the practical implications not just for baptism but for other areas of theology and practice as well.

It is interesting that Owen does not rest his argument on paedofaith or on a particular reading of the new covenant described in Jeremiah 31, or from a single text such as Colossians 2:11-12 as some might.[88] Significantly, he does not seem to have Roman Catholic errors particularly in mind as he develops this short treatise. Nor does he so anathematise non-paedobaptism that differences over this doctrine become a bar

[87] As Renihan, *Antipaedobaptism*, page 223 says, "All of the major works on baptism in the middle thirty years of the seventeenth century were written to interact with Tombes." He was "the sharpening agent for the Covenantal Paedobaptistic view" (page 210). Cf. pages 11-12.

[88] *Westminster Confession* 28.1 speaks of baptism as admission into the visible church, and it is perhaps also noteworthy that Owen does not use that language here (cf. its omission from the Savoy Declaration 29:1).

to fellowship or toleration.[89] Owen's respect for non-paedobaptists like John Bunyan is well-known.[90] What Owen is concerned with, however, is expounding the doctrine of infant baptism in a way that pays attention to the whole unified sweep of biblical revelation from creation to consummation, in order to demonstrate that Jesus does indeed secure and command the destiny of his children, from life's first cry until their final breath.

---

[89] For Owen's views on toleration see *Of Toleration: and the Duty of the Magistrate about Religion* in *The Works of John Owen: Volume 8*, pages 163-206 about which R. G. Lloyd, *John Owen: Commonwealth Puritan* (Pontypridd: Modern Welsh Publications, 1972), pages 62-63 comments, "it was the first work on toleration ever to be published in England while the author's own party was in power."

[90] See Toon, *God's Statesman*, pages 161-162. See also Bunyan's *Differences in Judgement about Water-Baptism no Bar to Communion* (London, 1673) in which he took an eirenic position towards paedobaptists in contrast to other 'Baptists' such as Kiffin, Paul, and Danvers. A similar debate about whether to allow those only baptised in infancy to be church members or to share in the Lord's Supper is active in baptistic circles today.

# Appendix 1: John Owen's *Of Infant Baptism*

Note: Page numbers from *The Works of John Owen: Volume 16* edited by W. H. Goold (Johnstone & Hunter, 1850-1853 // Edinburgh: T&T Clark, 1862 // Edinburgh: Banner of Truth, 1968) are placed in square brackets for ease of reference. I have updated verse references (changing Roman numerals). Footnotes are mine.

[258] I. THE question is not whether professing believers, Jews or Gentiles, not baptized in their infancy, ought to be baptized; for this is by all confessed.

II. Neither is it whether, in such persons, the profession of saving faith and repentance ought not to go before baptism. This we plead for beyond what is the common practice of those who oppose us.

Wherefore, testimonies produced out of authors, ancient or modern, to confirm these things, which consist with[91] the doctrine of infant baptism, are mere tergiversations,[92] that belong not to this cause at all; and so are all arguments produced unto that end out of the Scriptures.

III. The question is not whether all infants are to be baptized or not; for, according to the will of God, some are not to be baptized, even such whose parents are strangers from the covenant, But hence it will follow that some are to be baptized, seeing an exception confirms both rule and right.

IV. The question is only concerning the children or infant seed of professing believers who are themselves baptized. And, —

---

[91] i.e. are consistent with.

[92] That is, they evade the real question. Or as we might say, they are red herrings.

First, They by whom this is denied can produce no testimony of Scripture wherein their negation is formally or in terms included, nor any one asserting what is inconsistent with the affirmative; for it is weak beneath consideration to suppose that the requiring of the baptism of believers is inconsistent with that of their seed. But this is to be required of them who oppose infant baptism, that they produce such a testimony.

Secondly, No instance can be given from the Old or New Testament since the days of Abraham, none from the approved practice of the primitive church, of any person or persons born of professing, believing parents, who were themselves made partakers of the initial seal of the covenant, being then in infancy and designed to be brought up in the knowledge of God, who were not made partakers with them of the same sign and seal of the covenant.

Thirdly, A spiritual privilege once granted by God unto any cannot be changed, disannulled, or abrogated, without an especial divine [259] revocation of it, or the substitution of a greater privilege and mercy in the room of it; for, —

1. Who shall disannul what God hath granted? What he hath put together who shall put asunder? To abolish or take away any grant of privilege made by him to the church, without his own express revocation of it, is to deny his sovereign authority.

2. To say a privilege so granted may be revoked, even by God himself, without the substitution of a greater privilege and mercy in the room of it, is contrary to the goodness of God, his love and care unto his church, [and] contrary to his constant course of proceeding with it from the foundation of the world, wherein he went on in the enlargement and increase of its privileges until the coming of Christ. And to suppose it under the gospel is contrary to all his promises, the honour of Christ, and a multitude of express testimonies of Scripture.

Thus was it with the privileges of the temple and the worship of it granted to the Jews; they were not, they could not be, taken away without an express revocation, and the substitution of a more glorious spiritual temple and worship in their room.

But now the spiritual privilege of a right unto and a participation of the initial seal of the covenant was granted by God unto the infant seed of Abraham, Genesis 17:10, 12.

This grant, therefore, must stand firm for ever, unless men can prove or produce, —

1. An express revocation of it by God himself; which none can do either directly or indirectly, in terms or any pretense of consequence.

2. An instance of a greater privilege or mercy granted unto them in the room of it; which they do not once pretend unto, but leave the seed of believers, whilst in their infant state, in the same condition with those of pagans and infidels; expressly contrary to God's covenant.

All this contest, therefore, is to deprive the children of believers of a privilege once granted to them by God, never revoked, as to the substance of it, assigning nothing in its room; which is contrary to the goodness, love, and covenant of God, especially derogatory to the honour of Jesus Christ and the gospel.

Fourthly, They that have the thing signified have right unto the sign of it, or those who are partakers of the grace of baptism have a right to the administration of it: so Acts 10:47.

But the children of believers are all of them capable of the grace signified in baptism, and some of them are certainly partakers of it, namely, such as die in their infancy (which is all that can be said of professors): therefore they may and ought to be baptized. For, —

[260] 1. Infants are made for and are capable of eternal glory or misery, and must fall, dying infants, into one of these estates for ever.

2. All infants are born in a state of sin, wherein they are spiritually dead and under the curse.

3. Unless they are regenerated or born again, they must all perish inevitably, John 3:3. Their regeneration is the grace whereof baptism is a sign or token. Wherever this is, there baptism ought to be administered.

Fifthly, God having appointed baptism as the sign and seal of regeneration, unto whom he denies it, he denies the grace signified by it. Why is it the will of God that unbelievers and impenitent sinners should not be baptized? It is because, not granting them the grace, he will not grant them the sign. If, therefore, God denies the sign unto the infant seed of believers, it must be because he denies them the grace of it; and then all the children of believing parents dying in their infancy must, without hope, be eternally damned. I do not say that all must be so who are not baptized, but all must be so whom God would have not baptized.

But this is contrary to the goodness and law [love?] of God, the nature and promises of the covenant, the testimony of Christ reckoning them to the kingdom of God, the faith of godly parents, and the belief of the church in all ages.

It follows hence unavoidably that infants who die in their infancy have the grace of regeneration, and consequently as good a right unto baptism as believers themselves.

Sixthly, All children in their infancy are reckoned unto the covenant of their parents, by virtue of the law of their creation.

For they are all made capable of eternal rewards and punishments, as hath been declared.

But in their own persons they are not capable of doing good or evil.

It is therefore contrary to the justice of God, and the law of the creation of human kind, wherein many die before they can discern between their right hand and their left, to deal with infants any otherwise but in and according to the covenant of their parents; and that he doth so, see Romans 5:14.

Hence I argue, —

Those who, by God's appointment, and by virtue of the law of their creation, are, and must of necessity be, included in the covenant of their parents, have the same right with them unto the privileges of that covenant, no express exception being put in against them. This right it is in the power of none to deprive them of, unless they can change the law of their creation.

Thus it is with the children of believers with respect unto the [261] covenant of their parents, whence alone they are said to be holy, 1 Corinthians 7:14.

Seventhly, Christ is "the messenger of the covenant," Malachi 3:1, — that is, of the covenant of God made with Abraham; and he was the "minister of the circumcision for the truth of God, to confirm the promises made unto the fathers," Romans 15:8. This covenant was, that he would be "a God unto Abraham and to his seed."

Now if this be not so under the new testament, then was not Christ a faithful messenger, nor did confirm the truth of God in his promises.

This argument alone will bear the weight of the whole cause against all objections; for, —

> 1. Children are still in the same covenant with their parents, or the truth of the promises of God to the fathers was not confirmed by Christ.

> **2.** The right unto the covenant, and interest in its promises, wherever it be, gives right unto the administration of its initial seal, that is, to baptism, as Peter expressly declares, Acts 2:38, 39. Wherefore, —

The right of the infant seed of believers unto baptism, as the initial seal of the covenant, stands on the foundation of the faithfulness of Christ as the messenger of the covenant, and minister of God for the confirmation of the truth of his promises.

In brief, a participation of the seal of the covenant is a spiritual blessing. This the seed of believers was once solemnly invested in by God himself. This privilege he hath nowhere revoked, though he hath changed the outward sign; nor hath he granted unto our children any privilege or mercy in lieu of it now under the gospel, when all grace and privileges are enlarged to the utmost. His covenant promises concerning them, which are multiplied, were confirmed by Christ as a true messenger and minister; he gives the grace of baptism unto many of them, especially those that die in their infancy, owns children to belong unto his kingdom, esteems them disciples, appoints households to be baptized without exception. And who shall now rise up, and withhold water from them?

This argument may be thus further cleared and improved: —

Christ is "the messenger of the covenant," Malachi 3:1, – that is, the covenant of God with Abraham, Genesis 17:7; for, —

> **1.** That covenant was with and unto Christ mystical, Galatians 3:16; and he was the messenger of no covenant but that which was made with himself and his members.
>
> **2.** He was sent, or was God's messenger, to perform and accomplish the covenant and oath made with Abraham, Luke 1:72, 73.
>
> **3.** The end of his message and of his coming was, that those to whom he was sent might be "blessed with faithful

> Abraham," or that [262] "the blessing of Abraham," promised in the covenant, "might come upon them," Galatians 3:9, 14.

To deny this, overthrows the whole relation between the old testament and the new, the veracity of God in his promises, and all the properties of the covenant of grace, mentioned, 2 Samuel 23:5.

It was not the covenant of works, neither originally nor essentially, nor the covenant in its legal administration; for he confirmed and sealed that covenant whereof he was the messenger, but these he abolished.

Let it be named what covenant he was the messenger of, if not of this. Occasional additions of temporal promises do not in the least alter the nature of the covenant.

Herein he was the "minister of the circumcision for the truth of God, to confirm the promises made unto the fathers," Romans 15:8; that is, undeniably, the covenant made with Abraham, enlarged and explained by following promises. This covenant was, that God would be "a God unto Abraham and to his seed;" which God himself explains to be his infant seed, Genesis 17:12, — that is, the infant seed of every one of his posterity who should lay hold on and avouch that covenant as Abraham did, and not else. This the whole church did solemnly for themselves and their posterity; whereon the covenant was confirmed and sealed to them all, Exodus 24:7, 8. And every one was bound to do the same in his own person; which if he did not, he was to be cut off from the congregation, whereby he forfeited all privileges unto himself and his seed.

The covenant, therefore, was not granted in its administrations unto the carnal seed of Abraham as such, but unto his covenanted seed, those who entered into it and professedly stood to its terms.

And the promises made unto the fathers were, that their infant seed, their buds and offspring, should have an equal share in the covenant with them, Isaiah 22:24, 44:3, 61:9. "They are the seed of the blessed of the LORD, and their offspring with them," chap. 65:23. Not only themselves, who are the believing, professing seed of those who were blessed of the Lord, by a participation of the covenant, Galatians 3:9, but their offspring also, their brads, their tender little ones, are in the same covenant with them.

To deny, therefore, that the children of believing, professing parents, who have avouched God's covenant, as the church of Israel did, Exodus 24:7, 8 have the same right and interest with their parents in the covenant, is plainly to deny the fidelity of Christ in the discharge of his office.

It may be it will be said, that although children have a right to the covenant, or do belong unto it, yet they have no right to the initial seal of it. This will not suffice; for, —

> [263] 1. If they have any interest in it, it is either in its grace or in its administration. If they have the former, they have the latter also, as shall be proved at any time. If they have neither, they have no interest in it; — then the truth of the promises of God made unto the fathers was not confirmed by Christ.
>
> 2. That unto whom the covenant or promise doth belong, to them belongs the administration of the initial seal of it, is expressly declared by the apostle, Acts 2:38, 39, be they who they will.
>
> 3. The truth of God's promises is not confirmed if the sign and seal of them be denied; for that whereon they believed that God was a God unto their seed as well as unto themselves was this, that he granted the token of the covenant unto their seed as well as unto themselves. If this be taken away by Christ, their faith is overthrown, and the

promise itself is not confirmed but weakened, as to the virtue it hath to beget faith and obedience.

Eighthly, Particular testimonies may be pleaded and vindicated, if need be, and the practice of the primitive church.

## Appendix 2: Owen's letter to Lady Hartopp

Sir John and Lady Hartopp were particular friends of Owen, and for many years members of the small church in which he officiated during the closing years of his life. I include here the following letter from Pastor Owen to Lady Hartopp following the death of her baby daughter (probably Anne, who died in 1674), as an example of his pastoral use of the doctrine of covenant-infant salvation. We may not wish to emulate his style in every respect (encouraging a newly bereaved mother to "be cheerful" may not always be a wise or effective approach) but his earnest sincerity, compassion, and we might say even empathy (given his own history) do shine through. Can we see here something of his personal mental reasoning after the death of his own children?[93]

To Lady Elizabeth Hartopp,

Dear Madam, —

Every work of God is good; the Holy One in the midst of us will do no iniquity; and all things shall work together for good unto them that love him, even those things which at present are not joyous, but grievous; only his time is to be waited for, and his way submitted unto, that we seem not to be displeased in our hearts that he is Lord over us.

Your dear infant is in the eternal enjoyment of the fruits of all our prayers; for the covenant of God is ordered in all things, and sure. We shall go to her; she shall not return to us. Happy she was in this above us, that she had so speedy an issue

[93] I have updated the spelling and introduced paragraphing to aid the modern reader. The text can be found at the end of Andrew Thompson's biography of Owen in Goold (ed.), *The Works of John Owen: Volume 1,* pages cxvi-cxvii or P. Toon (ed.), *The Correspondence of John Owen (1616-1683)* (London: James Clarke, 1970), pages 157-158.

of sin and misery, being born only to exercise your faith and patience, and to glorify God's grace in her eternal blessedness.

My trouble would be great on the account of my absence at this time from you both, but that this also is the Lord's doing; and I know my own uselessness wherever I am. But this I will beg of God for you both that you may not faint in this day of trial, — that you may have a clear view of those spiritual and temporal mercies wherewith you are yet entrusted (all undeserved), — that sorrow of the world may not so overtake your hearts as to disenable to any duties, to grieve the Spirit, to prejudice your lives; for it tends to death. God in Christ will be better to you than ten children, and will so preserve your remnant, and to add to them, as shall be for his glory and your comfort. Only consider that sorrow in this case is no duty, it is an effect of sin, whose cure by grace we should endeavour. Shall I say, "Be cheerful"? I know I may. God help you to honour grace and mercy in a compliance therewith.

My heart is with you, my prayers shall be for you, and I am, dear madam, your most affectionate friend and unworthy pastor,

*J. Owen*

# Appendix 3: A liturgical introduction to infant baptism

To flesh out the practical implications of Owen's doctrine of infant baptism a little, I include below the introductory words that I use in Sunday services whenever an infant baptism takes place. As a pithy opening to that part of the proceedings it no doubt has its shortcomings, and I am not suggesting that it could be simply regurgitated in any context. But it reflects something of Owen's exegesis and approach, and since I have been asked for the wording on more than one occasion in the past I thought it might be a useful and appropriate appendix here.[94]

... Since the time of Abraham about 4000 years ago, God's people have been given an outward sign of admission into his covenant family. In the Old Testament the sign was circumcision; in the New Testament baptism is the sign of being part of God's people.

God said to Abraham in Genesis chapter 17 that the promises he signed and sealed through circumcision were for Abraham *and also for his children* – that he would be their God and they would be his people. Hence the children of believers were circumcised as babies under the Old Covenant.

This privilege has never expressly been taken away from our little ones. So, now that Christ has come to confirm the promises given to Abraham, children of believers under the New Covenant may receive baptism in the same way because again, as the Apostle Peter says, "*the promise is for you and for your children.*"

---

[94] See also the useful introductions to the two baptism services in *An English Prayer Book* (Oxford: OUP, 1994).

Baptism is the physical sign of a spiritual reality, which is that ***N*** here is a part of God's covenant family because she has been born to Christian parents. Her baptism today recognises that covenant reality, the spiritual privilege of being part of the household of faith.

But this does not mean, of course, that she is automatically going to heaven simply because we splash her with some water. As she matures she must believe and trust in the Lord Jesus to "cash in" (so to speak) on God's promise of eternal life. So we hope and pray that she is born again, and grows up to know and love Jesus as her Lord and saviour always.

So, using the words on the sheet, let's all pray for her now...

## For further reading:

These works sometimes take very different views on the theology of children, but together they give a sense of where the debate lies and what the major lines of argument have been.


M. J. Bunge (ed.), *The Child in Christian Thought* (Cambridge: Eerdmans, 2001)

J. Calvin, *Institutes of the Christian Religion* Book 4, Chapters 15 and 16.

R. H. Nash, *When a Baby Dies: Answers to Comfort Grieving Parents* (Grand Rapids: Zondervan, 1999)

M. T. Renihan, *Antipaedobaptism in the Thought of John Tombes: An Untold Story from Puritan England* (Auburn, MA: B & R Press, 2001)

L. B. Schenck, *The Presbyterian Doctrine of Children in the Covenant: An Historical Study of the Significance of Infant Baptism in the Presbyterian Church* (Phillipsburg, NJ: P&R, [1940] 2003)

T. R. Schreiner & S. D. Wright (eds.), *Believer's Baptism: Sign of the New Covenant in Christ* (Nashville: B&H Academic, 2006)

T. A. Sizemore, *Of Such is the Kingdom: Nurturing Children in the Light of Scripture* (Fearn, Ross-Shire: Christian Focus, 2000)

G. Strawbridge (ed.), *The Case for Covenantal Infant Baptism* (Phillipsburg, NJ: P&R, 2003)

B. B. Warfield, "The Polemics of Infant Baptism" and "The Development of the Doctrine of Infant Salvation" in *Studies in Theology, The Works of Benjamin B. Warfield: Volume 9* (Grand Rapids: Baker, reprinted 2003)

R. A. Webb, *The Theology of Infant Salvation* (Harrisonburg, Virginia: Sprinkle Publications, [1907] 2003)

# St. Antholin's Lectureship Charity Lectures

In or about 1560 the parish of St. Antholin, now absorbed into what is the parish of St. Mary-le-Bow in Cheapside and St Mary Alderbury, within the Cordwainer's Ward in the City of London, came into the possession of certain estates known as the "Lecturer's Estates". These were, it is believed, purchased with funds collected at or shortly after the date of the Reformation for the endowment of lectures of the Puritanical School of Divinity.

The first mention of the charity was an indenture, dated 24 June 1616, made between Richard Vane of the first part, the churchwardens of the parish of St. Antholin of the second part, and certain parishioners of the said parish of the third part.

Over the centuries the funds were not always used for the stated purpose, and in the first part of the nineteenth century a scheme was drawn up which revivified the lectureship, which was to consist of forty lectures to be given three times a year on the Puritan School of Divinity, the lecturer to receive one guinea per lecture. A further onerous requirement was that the lecturer had to be a beneficed Anglican, living within one mile of the Mansion House in the City of London.

Under such conditions the lectureship fell into disuse a long time ago, and it was not until 1987 that moves were put in hand with the Charity Commissioners to update the scheme. The first lecture under the new scheme was given in 1991.

## St. Antholin's Lectureship Charity Lectures

1991 *A Man for All Ministries: Richard Baxter 1651-1691,* J.I.Packer

1992 *The Recovery and Renewal of the Local Church – the Puritan Vision,* Geoffrey Cox

1993 *Evangelical Spirituality – Past Glories – Present Hopes – Future Possibilities,* Alister E. McGrath

1994 *"But We Preach Christ Crucified": The Cross of Christ in the Pastoral Theology of John Owen,* Gavin J. McGrath

1995 *Using the Shield of Faith – Puritan Attitudes to Combat with Satan,* Peter Jensen

1996 *An Anglican to Remember – William Perkins: Puritan Popularizer,* J.I.Packer

1997 *Pilgrim's Progress and Contemporary Evangelical Piety,* Bruce Winter

1998 *A Church 'Halfly Reformed' – the Puritan Dilemma,* Peter Adam

1999 *The Pilgrim's Principles: John Bunyan Revisited,* J.I.Packer

2000 *Conversion to Communion: Thomas Cranmer on a Favourite Puritan Theme,* Ashley Null

2001 *Word and Spirit: The Puritan-Quaker Debate,* Peter Adam

2002 *Usher on Bishops: A Reforming Ecclesiology,* Wallace Benn

2003 *Strangers to Correction: Christian Discipline and the English Reformation,* Peter Ackroyd

2004 *"Decalogue" Dod and his Seventeenth Century Bestseller: A Four Hundredth Anniversary Appreciation,* David Field

2005 *A Puritan Theology of Preaching,* Chad B. Van Dixhoorn

2006 *"To Bring Men to Heaven by Preaching" – John Donne's Evangelistic Sermons,* Peter Adam

2007 *1807 – 2007: John Newton and the Twenty-first Century,* Tony Baker